1979.

Happy ~~~~ ~~~~

from Clive & Diane
xxx   xxx

Happy

AUSTRALIA FAIR

A COUNTRY SCENE
Harold Herbert

AUSTRALIA FAIR

Poems and Paintings Selected by Douglas Stewart

URE SMITH

Sydney·Auckland·London·New York

First published in Australia 1974
by Ure Smith
a division of Paul Hamlyn Pty Limited
176 South Creek Road, Dee Why West, Australia, 2099

Designed and produced in Australia

Printed in Singapore

Jacket paintings: (front) *The Solitary Ramble*
by Julian Ashton, and (back) *Summer 1909*
by Sir Hans Heysen. Both reproduced with the
permission of the Trustees of the Art Gallery
of New South Wales.

CENTRAL AUSTRALIA
Sidney Nolan

Acknowledgments

Acknowledgments for permission to reprint poems in this anthology are due to Angus & Robertson (Publishers) Pty Ltd for the poems by A. B. Paterson, Mary Gilmore, Roderic Quinn, Christopher Brennan, Hugh McCrae, P. J. Hartigan ('John O'Brien'), Kenneth Slessor, Robert D. FitzGerald, A. D. Hope, Ronald McCuaig, Eve Langley, William Hart-Smith, Roland Robinson, Kenneth Mackenzie, Douglas Stewart, John Blight, David Campbell, Judith Wright, James McAuley, Rosemary Dobson, Nan McDonald, Nancy Keesing, Eric C. Rolls, Francis Webb, Randolph Stow, Les A. Murray and Geoffrey Lehmann; to Angus & Robertson and Lothian Publishing Co. Pty Ltd for the poem by Shaw Neilson; to Lothian Publishing Co. for the poem by Louis Esson; to Curtis Brown Ltd for the poem by Dorothea Mackellar; to the Hawthorn Press Pty Ltd for the poem by Paul Hasluck; to F. W. Cheshire Pty Ltd for the poem by Bruce Dawe; to Rigby Ltd for the poem by Colin Thiele.

Thanks are also due to Mr Oliver Streeton for permission to reproduce paintings by Sir Arthur Streeton; Mr W. G. Preston for paintings by Margaret Preston; the Australian National Gallery for paintings by Augustus Earle, Tom Roberts and Sir William Dobell; the New South Wales Art Gallery for paintings by Sydney Long, Julian Ashton and Albert Fullwood; the National Gallery of Victoria and Mrs Maurice Lambert for the painting by Sir George Lambert; Captain Brett Hilder for the painting by J. J. Hilder; Mrs O. Molvig for the painting by Jon Molvig; Mrs Veronica Rowan and Mr Mervyn Horton for the painting by David Strachan; Mrs J. Glad for the painting by Norman Lindsay; Arthur Murch for *The White Calf* and *Holiday;* Lloyd Rees for 'a bush scene'; Margaret Coen for *Christmas in Kuringai Chase;* John Perceval for *The Cornfield 1959* and *Girl Gathering Wattle in the Grampians;* the Art Gallery of South Australia and Sir Russell Drysdale for *Mullaloonah Tank;* the Perpetual Trustee Co. Ltd for the painting by Elioth Gruner; Mr Raven Macqueen for the painting by Kenneth Macqueen; and Mr David H. Heysen for the paintings by Sir Hans Heysen.

Contents

Poems and Paintings

Introduction

The plan of this anthology, as it was suggested to me by the publisher, was to select some of the best and most popular Australian poems and to try to match them with appropriate paintings by leading artists: so that at a single glance, as it were, we could see what the poets and the painters have thought about the country we live in.

In making the selection it was pleasant to come across a painting which happened really to illustrate one of the poems. It did not surprise me to find some Hans Heysen turkeys to place alongside Kenneth Mackenzie's 'Table-birds' with its delightful gobbling refrain, for I knew that Heysen had had a curious Turkey Period; but it was quite astonishing to take a close look at Conder's *The Farm, Richmond* and to realize that, besides matching the general pastoral charm' of James McAuley's 'At Rushy Lagoon', it actually had the poet's goose in it.

However, pleasing as these coincidences were, exact illustration of the poems was not the aim, but rather to find in the paintings a similarity or interesting variation of mood and theme. Julian Ashton's exquisite *A Solitary Ramble* does not illustrate Rosemary Dobson's 'Chance Met'; but it does suggest the lyrical morning mood of the poem, and the general ease and grace of Rosemary Dobson's writing. Similar conjunctions of atmosphere and mood, rather than of precise themes, may be found in the linking of Louis Esson with McCubbin, or Geoffrey Lehmann with John Perceval.

It was not really difficult on the whole (with the help of the publisher) to find poems and paintings that would keep harmonious company; and the reason for this is, of course, that both types of creative artists are concerned with the same environment and have gone through much the same historical development. Just as Conrad Martens had some difficulty in escaping from the conventions of English landscape to get a clear view of the Australian scene, yet sometimes succeeded brilliantly, and in any case made his own rich powerful statement, so, precisely, did Charles Harpur. Just as there was a breakthrough to a distinctively Australian school in the paintings of Tom Roberts, Streeton and Gruner, so did the bush balladists, Lawson and Paterson, with contributions on a higher plane from Mary Gilmore and Shaw Neilson, find an authentic Australian idiom. And just as many later painters have moved towards legend and heroic mythology, so has later poetry: Drysdale and Nolan have much in common with Judith Wright, David Campbell and (in his longer narrative poems) Francis Webb.

Here, then, is what the poets and the painters have thought about this vast and varied continent. I am sorry that, because of limitations of space, many of both are not able to be present on this occasion; but I trust that those who are represented will have something both attractive and significant to offer their readers and their viewers.

Douglas Stewart

A Midsummer Noon in the Australian Forest

NOT a sound disturbs the air,
There is quiet everywhere;
Over plains and over woods
What a mighty stillness broods!

All the birds and insects keep
Where the coolest shadows sleep;
Even the busy ants are found
Resting in their pebbled mound;
Even the locust clingeth now
Silent to the barky bough:
Over hills and over plains
Quiet, vast and slumbrous, reigns.

Only there's a drowsy humming
From yon warm lagoon slow coming:
'Tis the dragon-hornet—see!
All bedaubed resplendently,
Yellow on a tawny ground—
Each rich spot nor square nor round,
Rudely heart-shaped, as it were
The blurred and hasty impress there
Of a vermeil-crusted seal
Dusted o'er with golden meal.
Only there's a droning where
Yon bright beetle shines in air,
Tracks it in its gleaming flight
With a slanting beam of light,
Rising in the sunshine higher,
Till its shards flame out like fire.

Every other thing is still,
Save the ever-wakeful rill,
Whose cool murmur only throws
Cooler comfort round repose;
Or some ripple in the sea
Of leafy boughs, where, lazily,
Tired summer, in her bower
Turning with the noontide hour,
Heaves a slumbrous breath ere she
Once more slumbers peacefully.

O 'tis easeful here to lie
Hidden from noon's scorching eye,
In this grassy cool recess
Musing thus of quietness.

Charles Harpur

SILENT NOON
Arthur Streeton

Bell-birds

By channels of coolness the echoes are calling,
And down the dim gorges I hear the creek falling;
It lives in the mountain, where moss and the sedges
Touch with their beauty the banks and the ledges;
Through brakes of the cedar and sycamore bowers
Struggles the light that is love to the flowers.
And, softer than slumber, and sweeter than singing,
The notes of the bell-birds are running and ringing.

The silver-voiced bell-birds, the darlings of day-time,
They sing in September their songs of the May-time.
When shadows wax strong, and the thunder-bolts hurtle,
They hide with their fear in the leaves of the myrtle;
When rain and the sunbeams shine mingled together
They start up like fairies that follow fair weather,
And straightway the hues of their feathers unfolden
Are the green and the purple, the blue and the golden.

October, the maiden of bright yellow tresses,
Loiters for love in these cool wildernesses;
Loiters knee-deep in the grasses to listen,
Where dripping rocks gleam and the leafy pools glisten.
Then is the time when the water-moons splendid
Break with their gold, and are scattered or blended
Over the creeks, till the woodlands have warning
Of songs of the bell-bird and wings of the morning.

Welcome as waters unkissed by the summers
Are the voices of bell-birds to thirsty far-comers.
When fiery December sets foot in the forest,
And the need of the wayfarer presses the sorest,
Pent in the ridges for ever and ever,
The bell-birds direct him to spring and to river,
With ring and with ripple, like runnels whose torrents
Are toned by the pebbles and leaves in the currents.

Often I sit, looking back to a childhood
Mixt with the sights and the sounds of the wildwood,
Longing for power and the sweetness to fashion
Lyrics with beats like the heart-beats of passion—
Songs interwoven of lights and of laughters
Borrowed from bell-birds in far forest rafters;
So I might keep in the city and alleys
The beauty and strength of the deep mountain valleys,
Charming to slumber the pain of my losses
With glimpses of creeks and a vision of mosses.

Henry Kendall

A BUSH SCENE
Lloyd Rees

The Travelling Post Office

THE roving breezes come and go, the reed-beds sweep and sway,
The sleepy river murmurs low and loiters on its way,
It is the land of lots o' time along the Castlereagh. . . .

The old man's son had left the farm, he found it dull and slow,
He drifted to the great North-west, where all the rovers go.
"He's gone so long," the old man said, "he's dropped right out
    of mind,
But if you'd write a line to him I'd take it very kind;
He's shearing here and fencing there, a kind of waif and stray—
He's droving now with Conroy's sheep along the Castlereagh.

"The sheep are travelling for the grass, and travelling very slow;
They may be at Mundooran now, or past the Overflow,
Or tramping down the blacksoil flats across by Waddiwong;
But all those little country towns would send the letter wrong—
The mailman, if he's extra tired, would pass them in his sleep.
It's safest to address the note to 'Care of Conroy's sheep',
For five and twenty thousand head can scarcely go astray;
You write to 'Care of Conroy's sheep along the Castlereagh'."

By rock and ridge and riverside the western mail has gone
Across the great Blue Mountain Range to take that letter on.
A moment on the topmost grade, while open fire-doors glare,
She pauses like a living thing to breathe the mountain air,
Then launches down the other side across the plains away
To bear that note to "Conroy's sheep along the Castlereagh".

And now by coach and mailman's bag it goes from town to town,
And Conroy's Gap and Conroy's Creek have marked it
    "Further down".
Beneath a sky of deepest blue, where never cloud abides,
A speck upon the waste of plain the lonely mailman rides.
Where fierce hot winds have set the pine and myall boughs asweep
He hails the shearers passing by for news of Conroy's sheep.
By big lagoons where wildfowl play and crested pigeons flock,
By campfires where the drovers ride around their restless stock,
And past the teamster toiling down to fetch the wool away
My letter chases Conroy's sheep along the Castlereagh.

A. B. Paterson

MID-DAY
Sydney Long

Old Botany Bay

"I'm old
Botany Bay;
Stiff in the joints,
Little to say

I am he
Who paved the way,
That you might walk
At your ease to-day;

I was the conscript
Sent to hell
To make in the desert
The living well;

I bore the heat,
I blazed the track—
Furrowed and bloody
Upon my back.

I split the rock;
I felled the tree:
The nation was—
Because of me!"

Old Botany Bay
Taking the sun
From day to day . . .
Shame on the mouth
That would deny
The knotted hands
That set us high!

Mary Gilmore

VIEW FROM THE SUMMIT OF MOUNT YORK
Augustus Earle

Andy's Gone with Cattle

Our Andy's gone with cattle now—
Our hearts are out of order—
With drought he's gone to battle now
Across the Queensland border

He's left us in dejection now,
Our thoughts with him are roving;
It's dull on this selection now,
Since Andy went a-droving.

Who now shall wear the cheerful face
In times when things are slackest?
And who shall whistle round the place
When Fortune frowns her blackest?

Oh, who shall cheek the squatter now
When he comes round us snarling?
His tongue is growing hotter now
Since Andy crossed the Darling.

Oh, may the showers in torrents fall.
And all the tanks run over;
And may the grass grow green and tall
In pathways of the drover;

And may good angels send the rain
On desert stretches sandy;
And when the summer comes again
God grant 'twill bring us Andy.

Henry Lawson

THE WHITE CALF
Arthur Murch

The Fisher

ALL night a noise of leaping fish
Went round the bay,
And up and down the shallow sands
Sang waters at their play.

The mangroves drooped on salty creeks,
And through the dark,
Making a pale patch in the deep,
Gleamed, as it swam, a shark.

In streaks and twists of sudden fire
Among the reeds
The bream went by, and where they passed
The bubbles shone like beads.

All night the full deep drinking-song
Of nature stirred,
And nought beside, save leaping fish
And some forlorn night-bird.

No lost wind wandered down the hills
To tell of wide
Wild waterways; on velvet moved
The silky, sucking tide.

Deep down there sloped in shadowy mass
A giant hill;
And midway, mirrored in the tide,
The stars burned large and still.

The fisher, dreaming on the rocks,
Heard Nature say
Strange secret things that none may hear
Upon the beaten way,

And whisperings and wonder stirred,
And hopes and fears,
And sadness touched his heart, and filled
His eyes with star-stained tears:

And so, thrilled through with joy and love
And sweet distress,
He stood entranced, enchained by her
Full-breasted loveliness.

Roderic Quinn

THE FISHERMAN
Charles Conder

O Desolate Eves

O DESOLATE eves along the way, how oft,
despite your bitterness, was I warm at heart!
not with the glow of remember'd hearths, but warm
with the solitary unquenchable fire that burns
a flameless heat deep in his heart who has come
where the formless winds plunge and exult for aye
among the naked spaces of the world,
far past the circle of the ruddy hearths
and all their memories. Desperate eves,
when the wind-bitten hills turn'd violet
along their rims, and the earth huddled her heat
within her niggard bosom, and the dead stones
lay battle-strewn before the iron wind
that, blowing from the chill west, made all its way
a loneliness to yield its triumph room;
yet in that wind a clamour of trumpets rang,
old trumpets, resolute, stark, undauntable,
singing to battle against the eternal foe,
the wronger of this world, and all his powers
in some last fight, foredoom'd disastrous,
upon the final ridges of the world:
a war-worn note, stern fire in the stricken eve,
and fire thro' all my ancient heart, that sprang
towards that last hope of a glory won in defeat,
whence, knowing not sure if such high grace befall
at the end, yet I draw courage to front the way.

Christopher Brennan

BREAKING OF THE STORM
Conrad Martens

May

SHYLY the silver-hatted mushrooms make
  Soft entrance through,
And undelivered lovers, half awake,
  Hear noises in the dew.

Yellow in all the earth and in the skies,
  The world would seem
Faint as a widow mourning with soft eyes
  And falling into dream.

Up the long hill I see the slow plough leave
  Furrows of brown;
Dim is the day and beautiful: I grieve
  To see the sun go down.

But there are suns a many for mine eyes
  Day after day:
Delightsome in grave greenery they rise
  Red oranges in May.

Shaw Neilson

AUTUMN AFTERNOON
Hans Heysen

Fantasy

I LOVE to lie under the lemon
   That grows by the fountain;
To see the stars flutter and open
   Along the blue mountain.

To hear the last wonderful piping
   That rises to heaven,—
Six quavers to sum up delight in,
   And sorrow in seven—

To dream that the mythic wood-women,
   Each brown as the honey
The bees took their toll of from Hybla,
   On days that were sunny,

Come parting the hedge of my garden
   To dance a light measure
With soft little feet on the greensward,
   Peak-pointed for pleasure.

While Pan, on a leopard reclining,
   And birds on his shoulder,
Gives breath to a flute's wanton sighing
   Until their eyes smoulder.

Then, lo, in the pool of the valley
   Cries centaur to centaur,
As, plashing, they leap the white moonbuds
   The goddess had leant o'er.

They climb the steep sides of the chasm
   With hollowy thunder—
Whole cliffs at the stroke of their hoof-beats
   Split tumbling asunder!

They climb the steep sides of the chasm,
   And rush through the thicket
That chokes up the pathways that lead to
   My green garden-wicket.

They seize on the dancing wood-women,
   And kick poor Pan over
The back of his fat spotted leopard
   Amid the lush clover.

So I wake, and eagerly listen—
   But only the fountain,
Still sleeping and sobbing, complains at
   The foot of the mountain.

Hugh McCrae

FRUITS OF THE EARTH
Norman Lindsay

The Shearer's Wife

BEFORE the glare o' dawn I rise
To milk the sleepy cows, an' shake
The droving dust from tired eyes,
Look round the rabbit traps, then bake
    The children's bread.
There 's hay to stook, an' beans to hoe,
An' ferns to cut i' th' scrub below;
Women must work, when men must go
    Shearing from shed to shed.

I patch an' darn, now evening comes,
An' tired I am with labour sore,
Tired o' the bush, the cows, the gums,
Tired, but must dree for long months more
    What no tongue tells.
The moon is lonely in the sky,
Lonely the bush, an' lonely I
Stare down the track no horse draws nigh
    An' start . . . at the cattle bells.

Louis Esson

ON THE WALLABY TRACK
Frederick McCubbin

Said Hanrahan

"WE'LL all be rooned," said Hanrahan
In accents most forlorn
Outside the church ere Mass began
One frosty Sunday morn

The congregation stood about,
Coat-collars to the ears,
And talked of stock and crops and drought
As it had done for years.

"It's lookin' crook," said Daniel Croke;
"Bedad, it's cruke, me lad,
For never since the banks went broke
Has seasons been so bad."

"It's dry, all right," said young O'Neil,
With which astute remark
He squatted down upon his heel
And chewed a piece of bark.

And so around the chorus ran
"It's keepin' dry, no doubt."
"We'll all be rooned," said Hanrahan,
"Before the year is out.

"The crops are done; ye'll have your work
To save one bag of grain;
From here way out to Back-o'-Bourke
They're singin' out for rain.

"They're singin' out for rain," he said,
"And all the tanks are dry."
The congregation scratched its head,
And gazed around the sky.

"There won't be grass, in any case,
Enough to feed an ass;
There's not a blade on Casey's place
As I came down to Mass."

"If rain don't come this month," said Dan,
And cleared his throat to speak—
"We'll all be rooned," said Hanrahan,
"If rain don't come this week."

A heavy silence seemed to steal
On all at this remark;
And each man squatted on his heel,
And chewed a piece of bark.

"We want an inch of rain, we do,"
O'Neil observed at last;
But Croke "maintained" we wanted two
To put the danger past.

"If we don't get three inches, man,
Or four to break this drought,
We'll all be rooned," said Hanrahan,
"Before the year is out."

In God's good time down came the rain;
And all the afternoon
On iron roof and window-pane
It drummed a homely tune.

And through the night it pattered still,
And lightsome, gladsome elves
On dripping spout and window-sill
Kept talking to themselves.

It pelted, pelted all day long,
A-singing at its work,
Till every heart took up the song
Way out to Back-o'-Bourke.

And every creek a banker ran,
And dams filled overtop;
"We'll all be rooned," said Hanrahan,
"If this rain doesn't stop."

And stop it did, in God's good time:
And spring came in to fold
A mantle o'er the hills sublime
Of green and pink and gold.

And days went by on dancing feet,
With harvest-hopes immense,
And laughing eyes beheld the wheat
Nid-nodding o'er the fence.

And, oh, the smiles on every face,
As happy lad and lass
Through grass knee-deep on Casey's place
Went riding down to Mass.

While round the church in clothes genteel
Discoursed the men of mark,
And each man squatted on his heel,
And chewed his piece of bark.

"There'll be bush-fires for sure, me man,
There will, without a doubt;
We'll all be rooned," said Hanrahan,
"Before the year is out."

"John O'Brien"
(P. J. Hartigan)

My Country

THE love of field and coppice,
Of green and shaded lanes,
Of ordered woods and gardens
Is running in your veins;
Strong love of grey-blue distance,
Brown streams and soft, dim skies—
I know but cannot share it,
My love is otherwise.

I love a sunburnt country,
A land of sweeping plains,
Of ragged mountain ranges,
Of droughts and flooding rains.
I love her far horizons,
I love her jewel-sea,
Her beauty and her terror—
The wide brown land for me!

The stark white ring-barked forests,
All tragic to the moon,
The sapphire-misted mountains,
The hot gold hush of noon.
Green tangle of the brushes,
Where lithe lianas coil,
And orchids deck the tree-tops
And ferns the warm dark soil.

Core of my heart, my country!
Her pitiless blue sky,
When sick at heart, around us,
We see the cattle die—
But then the grey clouds gather,
And we can bless again
The drumming of an army,
The steady, soaking rain.

Core of my heart, my country!
Land of the Rainbow Gold,
For flood and fire and famine,
She pays us back threefold;
Over the thirsty paddocks,
Watch, after many days,
The filmy veil of greenness
That thickens as we gaze.

GOLDEN SUMMER
Sir Arthur Streeton

An opal-hearted country,
A wilful, lavish land—
All you who have not loved her,
You will not understand—
Though earth holds many splendours,
Wherever I may die,
I know to what brown country
My homing thoughts will fly.

Dorothea Mackellar

Country Towns

COUNTRY towns, with your willows and squares,
And farmers bouncing on barrel mares
To public-houses of yellow wood
With "1860" over their doors,
And that mysterious race of Hogans
Which always keeps General Stores. . . .

At the School of Arts, a broadsheet lies
Sprayed with the sarcasm of flies:
"The Great Golightly Family
Of Entertainers Here To-night"—
Dated a year and a half ago,
But left there, less from carelessness
Than from a wish to seem polite.

Verandas baked with musky sleep,
Mulberry faces dozing deep,
And dogs that lick the sunlight up
Like paste of gold—or, roused in vain
By far, mysterious buggy-wheels,
Lower their ears, and drowse again. . . .

Country towns with your schooner bees,
And locusts burnt in the pepper-trees,
Drown me with syrups, arch your boughs,
Find me a bench, and let me snore,
Till, charged with ale and unconcern,
I'll think it's noon at half-past four!

Kenneth Slessor

COUNTRY STREET
Harold Herbert

Week-end Miracle

THERE was nothing of this on Friday: here and there
a blossom perhaps; but air was only air,
not such immoderate honey as might bring
disrepute even upon Spring
if there should stagger with arm linked in his
a world which is not sick but fears it is.

Health is not healing, scars grown over, crust
upon the festered surface; it is out-thrust
of renewal from within—process of growth—
which aching and recovery both
are signs of, working through, like this white patch
of week-end miracle on tea-tree thatch.

And scarcity's not sickness: all between
the road and the ridge, coarse country and starved green
will not meet tax or interest, but defy
Monday's intolerable sky,
that the old urge towards living may prevail
as feathery globes that bleach the spurs like hail.

Robert D. FitzGerald

PATONGA
Margaret Preston

At Dyson's Swamp

TRUTH did not come in the laborious night
By lamp, or pen, or the deliberate clock;
But where the weeds were turning brown
And purple pigface and the yellowing dock
Clashed colour cymbals in my echoing brain.
—Heat on the pine trees and the still pond,
The sudden dart of tadpoles in a drain,
A whistling bird—from this impermanent arc
The spark of knowledge flashed. Mortality
Fell suddenly away, flesh from the bone.
Existence lay, a vast map seen by lightning,
With nutrient rivers and great ribs of stone.
—Beside a pond, where tall grass acrid in the sun
Sang of the season's end and tillage overgrown.

Paul Hasluck

BILLABONG
Margaret Preston

The Lamp and the Jar

YOU are that vessel full of holy oil:
Wisdom, unstirring in its liquid sleep,
Hoarded and cool, lucid and golden green,
Fills the pure flanks of the containing stone;
Here darkness mellows what the sunlit soil
To purposes unknown, for ends unseen,
Produced, and labour of unnumbered men.
All the unthinking earth with fret or toil
Reared, ripened, buried in the earth again,
Here lives, and living, waits: this source alone
Distils those fruitful tears the Muses weep.

And I, the lamp before the sacred ark,
The root of fire, the burning flower of light,
Draw from your loins this inexhaustible joy.
There the perpetual miracle of grace
Recurs, as, from its agony, the flame
Feeds the blind heart of the adoring dark;
And there the figures of our mystery,
The shapes of terror and inhuman woe,
Emerge and prophesy; there with the mark
Of blood upon his breast and on his brow,
An unknown king, with my transfigured face,
Bends your immortal body to his delight.

A. D. Hope

FLOWERS AND TWO HEADS
David Strachan

The Hungry Moths

POOR hungry white moths
That eat my love's clothing,
Who says very soon
Ye'll leave her with nothing,
Here under the moon
I make bold to persuade ye,
Ye may eat all her clothes
So ye leave me milady,
Poor
      hungry
            white
                  moths.

Ronald McCuaig

THE LOVERS
Jon Molvig

Native Born

In a white gully among fungus red
Where serpent logs lay hissing at the air,
I found a kangaroo. Tall, dewy, dead,
So like a woman, she lay silent there,
Her ivory hands, black-nailed, crossed on her breast,
Her skin of sun and moon hues, fallen cold.
Her brown eyes lay like rivers come to rest
And death had made her black mouth harsh and old.
Beside her in the ashes I sat deep
And mourned for her, but had no native song
To flatter death, while down the ploughlands steep
Dark young Camelli whistled loud and long,
"Love, liberty and Italy are all."
Broad golden was his breast against the sun.
I saw his wattle whip rise high and fall
Across the slim mare's flanks, and one by one
She drew the furrows after her as he
Flapped like a gull behind her, climbing high,
Chanting his oaths and lashing soundingly,
While from the mare came once a blowing sigh.
The dew upon the kangaroo's white side
Had melted. Time was whirling high around,
Like the thin woomera, and from heaven wide
God, the bull-roarer, made continuous sound.
Incarnate, lay my country by my hand:
Her long hot days, bushfires and speaking rains,
Her mornings of opal and the copper band
Of smoke around the sunlight on the plains.
Globed in fire bodies the meat-ants ran
To taste her flesh and linked us as we lay,
For ever Australian, listening to a man
From careless Italy, swearing at our day.
When, golden-lipped, the eagle-hawks came down
Hissing and whistling to eat of lovely her,
And the blowflies with their shields of purple brown
Plied hatching to and fro across her fur,
I burnt her with the logs, and stood all day
Among the ashes, pressing home the flame
Till woman, logs and dreams were scorched away,
And native with night, that land from where they came.

Eve Langley

THE STATION BOUNDARY
Albert Fullwood

Kangaroos

BROWN out of the brown tussock a darker brown
head rises as if thrust up cautiously on a pole.

A green bird on a feathering grass stem,
that bends under its weight, flutters

and sinks out of sight. It is the only disturbance
except for the reiterated clicking of castanets

and the fife-notes of insects.

One notices the head gone,
pulled down out of sight, like the vanished bird,

but all over the unfurled
map of the landscape minute brown

figures, dots, jump, all diminishing, yet
each pursuing

lines that intersect, making a maze
of crazy map-lines, meaningless angles.

The skin of the land is a deep fur
maddeningly come alive

with deliberate great fleas.

William Hart-Smith

KANGAROO HUNT
Edward Roper

The Tank

WHERE once the grey scrub's finches cried with thin
voices through the heat their "*nin-nin-nin*,"
bursts now the golden burgeon of this change
before the gibber plain, the pale blue range
Here to the fettlers' sunken water tank
the blacks came in; their three dun camels sank
down to their knees; the tall and bearded blacks
unslung the water-drums tied to the packs,
filled them, and called their camels and were gone
to where, out on the iron plain, led on
their lubras, children and lean dogs . . . to know
always the ranges' distant ebb and flow,
the wind-whorled sands that bare the parched white bone,
beneath their feet, the knife-sharp gibber-stone.

Roland Robinson

MULLALOONAH TANK
Russell Drysdale

Table-birds

THE match-bark of the younger dog sets fire to
an indignation of turkeys under the olives.
Scurf-wigged like senescent judges, drum-puffing desire,
they bloat their wattles, and the chorus gives
a purple biased judgment on the pup:
Trouble enough, pup, bloody trouble enough!

So much for morning and the sun's generous
flattery of the metal of their feathers.
Noon makes them somnolent, dusty, glad to drowse
the fly-slurred hours of midday August weather
in scooped hollows under the ripe trees
whose fruit sweetens them for the Christmas season.

The tilted sun, the craw's shrunk emptiness
wake them to stir their lice and strut again,
head back, tail spread, and dangling crest
and greedy, angered eye. . . . The spinsterly hen
blinks the lewd fan and frets among the grains,
knife-grey and sleek, hungrier, less restrained

by stifling turkey pride beneath the red
slap of the leering comb. But they submit.
The fan snaps to; head doubles over head—
and day's escape delineates them fitfully
like darkness clotted into nervous shapes
under the olives, in whose night they sleep.

Kenneth Mackenzie

TURKEYS
Hans Heysen

Christmas Bells

SEE them, the wild children
Running in their straight frocks
Of boldest orange and vermilion
All day in the sandstone rocks;

Where, sliding his crimson scales,
The black snake rustles and flows
Down the dry waterfalls
And smoky the blue wind blows,

Heady and hot from the hollow,
Telling what robe of fear
Scarlet and flaring yellow
The summer forest will wear.

"My children will never behave,
They have the sun's hot flesh,"
Cries the old mother in her cave;
"There on their long bare legs

"In the sun, in the smoke, in the threat,
Out from the cool stone shelves,
They dance all day in the heat
Like little bushfires themselves."

Douglas Stewart

CHRISTMAS IN KURINGAI CHASE
Margaret Coen

The Island

THE island is lost ground; an acre or two
in the realms of the sea. Is country
once loved of mother earth. Now, a whale's back
of wet mud, black, sliding back out of view
into the lost regions of a trackless sea;
and far, and farther away, as the tide's slack
takes up; is submerged, or part submerged
like a whale sounding in the shelving sea
—or could it be less noticed than a whale,
it is so small an island? Even the clouds have urged,
whipped it with rain, like spray, to go back to the sea;
crawl out the primeval monster, swishing a tail . . . .
There are such pleasures as becoming noticed, coming under the
    eye
of the lordly sun: an Island becoming an "I".

John Blight

SEASHORE
Kenneth MacQueen

On Frosty Days

ON frosty days, when I was young,
I rode out early with the men
And mustered cattle till their long
Blue shadows covered half the plain;

And when we turned our horses round,
Only the homestead's point of light,
Men's voices, and the bridles' sound,
Were left in the enormous night.

And now again the sun has set
All yellow and a greening sky
Sucks up the colour from the wheat—
And here's my horse, my dog and I.

David Campbell

MANAR LANDSCAPE
Elioth Gruner

South of My Days

South of my days' circle, part of my blood's country,
rises that tableland, high delicate outline
of bony slopes wincing under the winter,
low trees blue-leaved and olive, outcropping granite—
clean, lean, hungry country. The creek's leaf-silenced,
willow-choked, the slope a tangle of medlar and crab-apple
branching over and under, blotched with a green lichen;
and the old cottage lurches in for shelter.

O cold the black-frost night. The walls draw in to the warmth
and the old roof cracks its joints; the slung kettle
hisses a leak on the fire. Hardly to be believed that summer
will turn up again some day in a wave of rambler roses,
thrust its hot face in here to tell another yarn—
a story old Dan can spin into a blanket against the winter.
Seventy years of stories he clutches round his bones.
Seventy summers are hived in him like old honey.

Droving that year, Charleville to the Hunter,
nineteen-one it was, and the drought beginning;
sixty head left at the McIntyre, the mud round them
hardened like iron; and the yellow boy died
in the sulky ahead with the gear, but the horse went on,
stopped at the Sandy Camp and waited in the evening.
It was the flies we seen first, swarming like bees.
Came to the Hunter, three hundred head of a thousand—
cruel to keep them alive—and the river was dust.

Or mustering up in the Bogongs in the autumn
when the blizzards came early. Brought them down; we brought
    them
down, what aren't there yet. Or driving for Cobb's on the run
up from Tamworth—Thunderbolt at the top of Hungry Hill,
and I give him a wink. I wouldn't wait long, Fred,
not if I was you; the troopers are just behind,
coming for that job at the Hillgrove. He went like a luny,
him on his big black horse.

         Oh, they slide and they vanish
as he shuffles the years like a pack of conjurors' cards.
True or not, it's all the same; and the frost on the roof
cracks like a whip, and the back-log breaks into ash.
Wake, old man. This is winter, and the yarns are over.
No one is listening.
         South of my days' circle
I know it dark against the stars, the high lean country
full of old stories that still go walking in my sleep.

Judith Wright

THUNDERBOLT IN AN ENCOUNTER WITH THE POLICE AT PARADISE CREEK
Tom Roberts

At Rushy Lagoon

WET mirrors covering soft peat.
Swag-bellied graceful mares in foal.
Red-umber bulls on plashing feet
With mild white face and curly poll

Crutching time; each heavy ewe
Is trimmed and slides off down the chute.
The mountains are cut out in blue.
An opalescent sky is mute.

Ducks loiter. Children play before tea.
In the home paddock a lone goose
Follows the cows for company.
It is a world of sense and use.

James McAuley

THE FARM, RICHMOND
Charles Conder

Bert Schultz

BERT SCHULTZ on his West Coast farm
Eases backwards through the doorway of his truck,
And the cabin grows around him, the wheel
Finds comfort in a padded stomach rut.
Bert Schultz in motion is a monstrous forward shoot
Because he crushes the accelerator like a toadstool
Under his six-pound boot.

Bert Schultz on his West Coast farm
Wears braces like railway tracks
That start from button boulders,
Junction in the middle of his back
And climb over the mountains of his shoulders.

Bert Schultz in his West Coast town
Has a fence-post arm to buttress up the bar,
Spins a thimble schooner in the stale-smelling ebb,
Talks about sheep and the way prices are.

The glass hidden in his ham-bone fist,
An hour later he still talks farm,
While the flies tip and veer
In the tangle of the wire sprouting on his arm.

Bert Schultz down a West Coast street
Makes me certain Eyre Peninsula
Has taken to its legs,
And is walking round the place on tree-stump feet;
Makes me feel the steel of yaccas,
And the supple punch of mallee,
And the thirsty tug of eighteen-gallon kegs.

Bert Schultz knows something of tractor oils and sumps,
Sheep dogs and petrol pumps
And an occasional punch to the chin.
But when he laughs like a shaking mountain,
Or gullies his face badly with a grin,
He opens suddenly and lets you in.

Colin Thiele

THE BILLY BOY
William Dobell

Chance Met

SWING back the gate till it stumbles over the furrows
Where the plough swerves close to the fence and the brown earth
    crumbles
From mountains created with tossed up tussocks, to valleys
Runnelled with rivers of rain.
The drops hang bright on the wires, the diligent spider
Worked shifts all night to set up his house by sunrise
Between the hinge, rusted with rain, and the latch.

Who went before through the gate—this affable stranger
Who touches the topmost rail and leans to dazzle,
Spinning his hat for greeting? Morning,
Golden and rakish, who stole his shirt from the scarecrow
To shroud the fire at heart. Good Morning
Swing back the gate, good fellow.
Swing back the gate! There is nobody there. The sunlight
In golden footprints runs up the ridge of the hill.

Rosemary Dobson

THE SOLITARY RAMBLE
Julian Ashton

65

The White Eagle

EVENING falls soon in the hills across the river,
Moving dark where the treetops gleamed a moment before,
Chilling to steel the lazy sweep of the reaches,
And at last, salt-cold, comes rippling in to our shore,

Where the gulls long since wheeled up and went flashing seaward,
With the tide's first ebb deserting the threatened land;
And the shag no longer sits where the bleaching driftwood
Thrusts from the slate-blue mud and damp white sand.

And the shadow climbs, and the clamorous gold-green thickets
Grow shrill with a brief unease that falls dulled to rest;
The thrush drops his gentle head, as in secret listening
To the freshets of silver locked in his soft grey breast.

And the lyre-bird too, that gay and skilful fellow,
Who set the dawn-fogged dew of the bush alight
With the opal glow of his soul and his art's rich cunning,
Can find no song for this other grey of night.

Now far and steeply above us the dusk has swallowed
The glint of the wiry grass that the boulders strew,
Echoing no more to the thronged black currawongs' calling
Where the rose-limbed trees twist out to pattern the blue.

But the light turns blazing at bay in its last high fortress
And the walls of yellow sandstone with glory run,
A crown for the night-gulfed slopes, and a golden footstool
For the lord of the rocks and the champion of the sun.

Stainless he rides on the swimming air, and below him
Roll the vast dim sea and the splendour of the world;
And the strength of his wing will be gilded, his breast still
        blinding
When the citadel falls with its blackened banners furled.

Tomorrow I too must be dropping down the river
With the screams of the flickering gulls for my parting words,
And in the thick town I shall be often thinking
Of the great hill darkening here, and my quiet birds.

I shall wish them all a still dusk and safe dreaming,
But the lift of my heart will follow my shining one
Where the high bright cliffs rise burning, and he beyond them,
All his white beauty warm in the eye of the sun.

Nan McDonald

AT CLOSE OF DAY
J. J. Hilder

Bread

I MAKE man's ancient food
That at blood's temperature
Gathered its own life,
Began to seethe and stir.

I plunge my fists within
Resilient dough for bread,
The living, leavened stuff
Fragrant and moist to knead

Takes shape now from my hand,
Its warmth of growing yeast
Springs from the palm pressed in
And curls back to resist.

My atavistic hands
Find an old skill to throw
And press and curve and turn
And shape the living dough.

I set the bread to rise
And hear the smallest sound
Beneath the muslin cloth
That covers it around.

It is the sound of life
From dough that warmed the hand
And took blood's heat to grow.
I shape the loaves, they stand

Again to rise before
Their baking into food—
Bread that is symbol of
Plain goodness, life and God.

All generations of women
Who ground the flour for bread,
And set it by their ovens
And curved strong hands to knead,

How intimately they knew
Whence man's true symbols come:
The seed, the yeast, the bread,
The child swelling the womb.

Nancy Keesing

HOLIDAY
Arthur Murch

Sheaf-tosser

THE lone crow caws from the tall dead gum:
Caw. Caw. Caw-diddle-daw.
And judges the stack with one watery eye,
Then turns the other to fix its lie.
Caw. Caw. Caw-diddle-daw.
There are four tiers of sheaves on the wagon yet
And one more loaded is standing by;
My arms are aching and I'm dripping sweat
But the sun is three axe-handles in the sky
And I must toss sheaves till dark.

It is fourteen feet from the ground to the eaves:
Caw. Caw. Caw-diddle-daw.
And two feet six to the third roof row,
Six feet high stands the load below:
Caw. Caw. Caw-diddle-daw.
Ten feet six now must I pitch,
Into the centre of the stack I throw
To the turner and the short-handled fork with which
He thrusts sheaves to the builder in monotonous flow,
Butts out and long-side down.

There are twenty-five crows on the old dry gum:
Caw. Caw. Caw-diddle-daw.
Thirteen on one branch and twelve on the other
And each one calls as loud as his brother,
Caw. Caw. Caw-diddle-daw.
My hands are blistered, my sore lips crack
And I wonder whether the turner would smother
If a hard throw knocked him off the stack
And a few sheaves slipped on top? But there'd come another
And I'd still toss sheaves.

There are thousands of crows on the gaunt white gum:
Caw. Caw. Caw-diddle-daw.
The reds are pale in the western sky
And the stack is more than sixty feet high:
Caw. Caw. Caw-diddle-daw.
My fork grows heavy as the light grows dim.
There are five sheaves left but I've fear of a whim
That one of the crows has an evil eye
And the five sheaves left will be there when I die,
For each bird's forgotten how to fly
Till he drives out my soul with the force of his cry:
Caw. Caw. Caw. Caw.
Caw. Caw. Caw. Caw.

Eric Rolls

THE CORNFIELD 1959
John Perceval

Elegy for Drowned Children

WHAT does he do with them all, the old king:
Having such a shining haul of boys in his sure net,
How does he keep them happy, lead them to forget
The world above, the aching air, birds, spring?

Tender and solicitous must be his care
For these whom he takes down into his kingdom one by one
—Why else would they be taken out of the sweet sun,
Drowning towards him, water plaiting their hair?

Unless he loved them deeply how could he withstand
The voices of parents calling, calling like birds by the water's
        edge,
By swimming-pool, sand-bar, river-bank, rocky ledge,
The little heaps of clothes, the future carefully planned?

Yet even an old acquisitive king must feel
Remorse poisoning his joy, since he allows
Particular boys each evening to arouse
From leaden-lidded sleep, softly to steal

Away to the whispering shore, there to plunge in,
And fluid as porpoises swim upward, upward through the
        dividing
Waters until, soon, each back home is striding
Over thresholds of welcome dream with wet and moonlit skin.

Bruce Dawe

BY TRANQUIL WATERS
Sydney Long

Strange Fruit

SUICIDE of the night—ah, flotsam:
(the great
poised thunderous breaker of darkness rearing above you,
and your bones awash, in the shallows, glimmering, stony,
like gods of forgotten tribes, in forgotten deserts)

take care. Take care. For your campfire falters, and firelight
folds, and will clamp around you its charcoal calyx,
and already for many hours your eyes (my terror)
have drowned in deep waters of dream, till I grow fearless.

(Embers of crocodiles love you from the mangroves.
Dingo ears yearn, yearn towards your tranquil breathing.)

Day and the firelight guard you from harm so darkly
rehearsed, removing me far; for by day I dread you,
fearing your quester's ear, that might interpret
what sings in my blood; your eye, that might guess my fever.

But so long as the harsh light lasts, I stalk your horses'
desolate spoor: a statue among the anthills,
should you look back; and prowling—and yearning, yearning,
howl out my grief and grievance, and burn in fever.

(Embers of crocodiles love you from the mangroves.
Dingo ears suck the wind for your tranquil breathing.)

I am the country's station; all else is fever.
Did we ride knee to knee down the canyons, or did I dream it?
They were lilies of dream we swam in, parrots of myth
we named for each other, "since no one has ever named them . . ."

Alone for an hour, in a thicket, I reached for strange fruit.

Now you sleep by the fire. And these are my true eyes
that glare from the swamps. And the rattling howl in the gullies
is my true voice. That cries: *You shall try strange fruit.*

Randolph Stow

ANTHILLS ON ROCKY PLAINS
Russell Drysdale

Lament for the Country Soldiers

THE king of honour, louder than of England
Cried on the young men to a gallant day
And ate the hearts of those who would not go

For the gathering ranks were the Chosen Company
That each man in his lifetime seeks, and finds,
Some for an hour, some beyond recall.

When to prove their life, they set their lives at risk
And in the ruins of horizons died
One out of four, in the spreading rose of their honour

They didn't see the badge upon their hat
Was the ancient sword that points in all directions,
The symbol hacked the homesteads even so.

The static farms withstood it to the end,
The galloping telegrams ceasing, the exchanges
Ringing no more in the night of the stunned violin,

And in the morning of insult, the equal remember
Ribaldry, madness, the wire jerking with friends,
Ironic salutes for the claimants of the fox-hunt

As, camped under tin like rabbiters in death's gully
They stemmed the endless weather of grey men and steel
And, first of all armies, stormed into great fields.

But it was a weight beyond speech, the proven nation
On beasts and boys. Newborn experiment withered.
Dull horror rotting miles wide in the memory of green.

Touching money, the white feather crumpled to ash,
Cold lies grew quickly in the rank decades
As, far away, the ascendant conquered courage,

And we debauched the faith we were to keep
With the childless singing on the morning track,
The Sportsmen's Thousand leaping on the mountains,

Now growing remote, beneath their crumbling farms,
In the district light, their fading companies
With the king of honour, deeper than of England

Though the stones of increase glitter with their names.

Les. A. Murray

A SERGEANT OF THE LIGHT HORSE
G. W. Lambert

Pear-country

WE are the old men of the pear country, minds
Distorted by pear, the folds of our cortex curving
Over in pear-gullies, forearms thick as pear-trunk.
We walk through phantom groves in our night-shirts
Wander holding a candle through pear-nightmares,
Calling for our lost cattle, the roan herds chewing
Amongst the temples of cactus, the green embankments.
Our nights grow trees with a hundred eyeless heads,
Leaning at all angles, ears cocked to the wind.

Our cattle when we saw them were small, tough beasts
A strange new race which bred amongst the thorns
With horny palates and nimble, dodging gait.
We tried to muster them, our horses jumping
And crashing in the pear, cracking our whips
On pads while the cattle vanished in green tunnels
In fear we walked the moonlit track to the privy
Striking blindly with sticks at slits in the moonlight,
The small death-adders who swarmed amongst the cactus.
We bred and we hacked in the great pear-loneliness,
Our manners crabbed, our lips always moving softly
As we dug and cut and burned, our children half-starved,
Close neighbours total strangers never seen
Through walls of cactus, the world a flimsy patch
Of daylight at the end of a telescope
Of pear, our boundaries, old wire fences lost
In the tangle of spines, creeks and even hills
Lost, no one quite knew where. We cut, we slept,
With only one track out we could keep clear,
Always afraid that one day we would lose it
And the town would forget us and we would turn to green pulp.
At night from our verandas we would stare
Into thorn-darkness looking for neighbours' lights
And saw just pear regiments polished in the moonlight.
And when the cactoblastis came the pear
Collapsed, a moth winged through the dropping arcades,
And we blinked at the sky and country stretching for miles,
Our houses rusting and unpainted standing
In acres of pear-slime and melting branches.
We slid and waded through the slush to shake
The hands of neighbours whom we had forgotten,
Our tongues stiff and our mouths sore from the pear,
And there were dances every night, our children
Skidding in pumps to foxtrots from gramophones,
But we stood beyond the hissing pressure lamps,
Not speaking, thinking still in pear-country,
Picking up thorns and splitting them with our fingers.

Geoffrey Lehmann

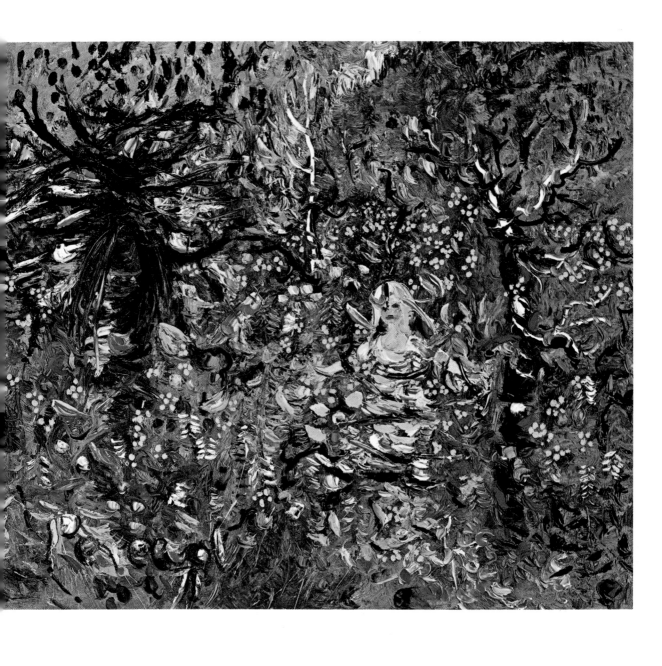

GIRL GATHERING WATTLE IN THE GRAMPIANS
John Perceval

"The Room" (from Leichhardt in Theatre)

MOVES to the window, stares at eddying dust,
And thinks of dust. Of Gilbert. The pale face
Stamped by the marvellous speed, and covered quickly
Because the eyes were open, shows itself.
Has Gilbert found the source? or do his bones,
Forever at war with death,
Trudge nightly towards Port Essington, till dawn
Chains them again to stone?
                              A question stares
Relentless from the dust, the answer traces
Legends of fright upon his brain, he turns
Swiftly back to the mirror and, as one
Aloof, for a moment watches fear at work.

But now they close round him in the room:
The question eats its way until the heart
Crumbles beneath its golden arrogance
And he must answer.
                          Savage and at bay!
Fronting the mirror and the tamed grey hound
Whimpering in the glass: "No back is broken
Under a rod of lies." The painted shell:
"Deception is all distance to the sea."
Still, still, the dust. "Shall a man go grazy for the kiss
Of thirst upon his throat? Shall he explore
Time after time this death's-head continent,
Probe the eye-sockets, skinless cavities,
Till the brain sweats from his skull, his hands contract,
And bone probes bone at length; bone lifted to cheek
Knows the flesh dwindling, blasted by such a love?"

Falls silent and betrayed. The walls slope out,
Space bunts at the doorway. Wash of darkness
Save for three shining things. The Furies circle:
Desert with bleached eyes, mountain with the hawk's mouth,
Sea with her witching falseness; cordon him.
He is taken, stripped, and bound.

Francis Webb

80